A Scolar Press Facsimile

THE
SHEPHERD'S WEEK

John Gay

1714

Printed and published in Great Britain by
The Scolar Press Limited, Menston, Yorkshire
and 39 Great Russell Street, London WC1

This facsimile first published 1969
Reprinted 1973

ISBN
0 85417 038 3
(Cloth)

ISBN
0 85417 965 8
(Paperback)

Introductory Note

The Shepherd's Week was the product of a literary genre which owed its revival in England to Ambrose Phillips's *Pastorals*, which first appeared in 1708. The literary theory underlying the revival of the pastoral eclogue can be traced in four numbers of the *Guardian* (22, 23, 28, 30), believed to be the work of Thomas Tickell (whose *Kensington Garden* (1722) enjoyed considerable popularity), though the first may have been by Addison.

> It is easy to be observed that these rules are drawn from what our Countrymen Spencer and Phillips have performed in this way . . . As far as our language would allow them, they have formed a pastoral style according to the Doric of Theocritus, in which I dare not say they have excelled Virgil; but I may be allowed, for the honour of our language, to suppose it more capable of that pretty rusticity than the Latin.
>
> (*Guardian*, No. 30, April 15, 1713)

Phillips's *Pastorals* practise, furthermore, much of the theory in William Walsh's *Essay on Pastoral Poetry* (1697), and his slavish adherence to what was clearly a barren theory earned him the contempt first of Pope, and then Gay, whose burlesque of the pastoral in the *Shepherd's Week*, with its preposterous 'Proeme', can be seen as an attempt to discredit Phillips. (See further H. Trowbridge, *Modern Language Quarterly*, V, 1944, 79–88.)

The popularity of Gay's poem during the eighteenth century may be judged from the number of times it was reprinted: second edition, 1714; 1721; Dublin, 1728; London, 1728 (fourth edition); 1742 (fifth edition); Edinburgh, 1760. The text was reprinted, with an introduction by H. F. B. Brett-Smith, in 1924. Gay's *Works* first appeared at Dublin in 1770 (4 vols.), with a London reprint in 1772, and an edition of the *Poetical, Dramatic, and Miscellaneous Works* (with Johnson's life) appeared in 1795. The standard modern edition is that of G. C. Faber, *The Poetical Works*, with a detailed bibliography (1926).

Frontispice.   Lud. Du Guernier inv. et sculp.

THE

SHEPHERD's WEEK.

IN SIX

PASTORALS.

By Mr J. GAY.

——————— *Libeat mihi ſordida rura,*
Atque humiles habitare Caſas. —— Virg.

LONDON,

Printed : And Sold by FERD. BURLEIGH in
Amen-Corner. M DCCXIV.

THE

PROEME

To the Courteous

READER.

REAT *Marvell hath it been,* (*and that not unworthily*) *to diverse worthy Wits, that in this our Island of* Britain, *in all rare Sciences so greatly abounding, more especially in all kinds of Poesie highly flourishing, no Poet* (*though otherways of notable Cunning in Roundelays*) *hath hit on the right simple Eclogue after the true ancient guise of* Theocritus, *before this mine Attempt.*

Other Poet travailing in this plain High-way of Pastoral know I none. Yet, certes, such it behoveth a Pastoral to be, as Nature in the Country affordeth; and

A 3 *the*

The PROEME.

the *Manners* also *meetly copied from the* ruftical *Folk therein. In this also my* Love *to my native Country* Britain *much pricketh me forward, to defcribe aright the* Manners *of our own honeft and laborious* Plough-men, *in no wife fure more unworthy a* Britifh *Poet's imitation, than thofe of* Sicily *or* Arcadie ; *albeit, not ignorant I am, what a* Rout *and* Rabblement *of Critical* Gallimawfry *hath been made of late Days by certain young* Men *of infipid* Delicacy, *concerning, I wift not what,* Golden Age, *and other outragious Conceits, to which they would confine* Paftoral. *Whereof, I avow, I account nought at all, knowing no* Age *fo juftly to be inftiled* Golden, *as this of* our Soveraign Lady Queen ANNE.

This idle Trumpery *(only fit for Schools and Schoolboys) unto that ancient* Dorick *Shepherd* Theocritus, *or his* Mates, *was never known ; he rightly, throughout his fifth* Idyll, *maketh his Louts give foul Language, and behold their Goats at Rut in all Simplicity.*

Ὠπόλ☉ ὄκκ᾿ ἐσορῇ τὰς μηκάδας οἶα βατεῦντι
Τάκεται ὀφθαλμὼς ὅτι ὐ τράγ☉ αὐτὸς ἔγεντο.
                                                          Theoc.

Verily, as little Pleafance *receiveth a true homebred* Taft, *from all the fine finical new-fangled Fooleries of this gay* Gothic *Garniture, wherewith they fo nicely bedeck their* Court Clowns, *or* Clown Courtiers, *(for, which to call them rightly, I wot not) as would a prudent* Citizen *journeying to his Country Farms, fhould he find them occupied by People of this motley Make, inftead of plain downright hearty cleanly Folk ; fuch as be now Tenants to the wealthy* Burgeffes *of this Realme.*

                                                        Further-

The PROEME.

Furthermore, it is my Purpose, gentle Reader, to set before thee, as it were a Picture, or rather lively Landscape of thy own Country, just as thou mightest see it, didest thou take a Walk into the Fields at the proper Season: even as Maister Milton hath elegantly set forth the same.

As one who long in populous City pent,
Where Houses thick and Sewers annoy the Aire,
Forth issuing on a Summer's Morn to breathe
Among the pleasant Villages and Farms
Adjoin'd, from each thing met conceives Delight;
The Smell of Grain or tedded Grass or Kine
Or Dairie, each rural Sight, each rural Sound.

Thou wilt not find my Shepherdesses idly piping on oaten Reeds, but milking the Kine, tying up the Sheaves, or if the Hogs are astray driving them to their Styes. My Shepherd gathereth none other Nosegays but what are the growth of our own Fields, he sleepeth not under Myrtle shades, but under a Hedge, nor doth he vigilantly defend his Flocks from Wolves, because there are none, as Maister Spencer well observeth.

Well is known that since the *Saxon* King
Never was Wolf seen, many or some
Nor in all *Kent* nor in Christendom.

For as much, as I have mentioned Maister Spencer, soothly I must acknowledge him a Bard of sweetest Memorial. Yet hath his Shepherd's Boy at some times raised his rustick Reed to Rhimes more rumbling than rural.

A 4   *Diverse*

The PROEME.

Diverse grave Points also hath he handled of Churchly Matter and Doubts in Religion daily arising, to great Clerkes only appertaining. What liketh me best are his Names, indeed right simple and meet for the Country, such as Lobbin, Cuddy, Hobbinol, Diggon, *and others, some of which I have made bold to borrow. Moreover, as he called his Eclogues, the Shepherd's Calendar, and divided the same into the twelve Months, I have chosen (paradventure not overrashly) to name mine by the Days of the Week, omitting* Sunday *or the* Sabbath, *Ours being supposed to be Christian Shepherds, and to be then at Church worship. Yet further of many of Maister* Spencer's *Eclogues it may be observed; though Months they be called, of the said Months therein, nothing is specified; wherein I have also esteemed him worthy mine Imitation.*

That principally, courteous Reader, whereof I would have thee to be advertised, (seeing I depart from the vulgar Usage) is touching the Language of my Shepherds; which is, soothly to say, such as is neither spoken by the country Maiden nor the courtly Dame; nay, not only such as in the present Times is not uttered, but was never uttered in Times past; and, if I judge aright, will never be uttered in Times future. It having too much of the Country to be fit for the Court; too much of the Court to be fit for the Country, too much of the Language of old Times to be fit for the Present, too much of the Present to have been fit for the Old, and too much of both to be fit for any time to come. Granted also it is, that in this my Language, I seem unto my self, as a London *Mason, who calculateth his Work for a Term of Years, when he buildeth with old Materials upon a Ground-rent*

that

The PROEME.

that is not his own, which soon turneth to Rubbish and
Ruins. For this point, no Reason can I alledge, only
deep learned Ensamples having led me thereunto.

But here again, much Comfort ariseth in me, from
the Hopes, in that I conceive, when these Words in the
course of transitory Things shall decay, it may so hap,
in meet time that some Lover of Simplicity shall arise,
who shall have the Hardiness to render these mine E-
clogues into such more modern Dialect as shall be then
understood, to which end, Glosses and Explications of un-
couth Pastoral Terms are annexed.

Gentle Reader, turn over the Leaf, and entertain
thyself with the Prospect of thine own Country, limned
by the painful Hand of

thy Loving Countryman

JOHN GAY.

P R O-

PROLOGUE.

To the Right Honourable the

L^d Viſcount _Bolingbroke._

O, I who erſt beneath a Tree
Sung _Bumkinet_ and _Bowzybee_,
And _Blouzelind_ and _Marian_
bright,
In Apron blue or Apron white,
Now write my Sonnets in a Book,
For my good Lord of _Bolingbroke._

As

PROLOGUE.

As Lads and Lasses stood around
To hear my Boxen Haut-boy sound,
Our *Clerk* came posting o'er the Green
With doleful Tidings of the *Queen*;
That Queen, he said, to whom we owe
Sweet *Peace that maketh Riches flow*;
That *Queen* who eas'd our Tax of late,
Was dead, alas!---and lay in State.

At this, in Tears was *Cic'ly* seen,
Buxoma tore her Pinners clean,
In doleful Dumps stood ev'ry Clown,
The Parson rent his Band and Gown.

For me, when as I heard that Death
Had snatch'd *Queen ANNE* to *Elzabeth*,
I broke my Reed, and sighing swore
I'd weep for *Blouzelind* no more.

While

P R O L O G V E.

While thus we ſtood as in a ſtound,
And wet with Tears, like Dew, the Ground,
Full ſoon by Bonefire and by Bell
We learnt our Liege was paſſing well.
A ſkilful Leach, (ſo God him ſpeed)
They ſaid had wrought this bleſſed Deed,
This Leach *Arburthnot* was yclept
Who many a Night not once had ſlept;
But watch'd our gracious Sov'raign ſtill,
For who cou'd reſt when ſhe was ill?
Oh, may'ſt thou henceforth ſweetly ſleep.
Sheer, Swains, oh ſheer your ſofteſt Sheep
To ſwell his Couch; for well I ween,
He ſav'd the Realm who ſav'd the Queen.

Quoth I, pleaſe God, I'll hye with Glee
To Court, this *Arburthnot* to ſee.
I ſold my Sheep and Lambkins too,
For ſilver Loops and Garment blue;

My

PROLOGUE.

My boxen Haut-boy fweet of found,
For Lace that edg'd mine Hat around;
For *Lightfoot* and my Scrip I got
A gorgeous Sword, and eke a Knot.

So forth I far'd to Court with fpeed,
Of Soldier's Drum withouten Dreed;
For Peace allays the Shepherd's Fear
Of wearing Cap of Granadier.

There faw I Ladies all a-row
Before their Queen in feemly Show.
No more I'll fing *Buxoma* brown,
Like Goldfinch in her *Sunday* Gown;
Nor *Clumſilis*, nor *Marian* bright,
Nor Damfel that *Hobnelia* hight.
But *Lanſdown* freſh as Flow'r of *May*,
And *Berkely* Lady blithe and gay,

And

And *Anglesey* whose Speech exceeds
The Voice of Pipe, or oaten Reeds;
And blooming *Hide*, with Eyes so rare,
And *Montague* beyond compare.
Such Ladies fair wou'd I depaint
In Roundelay or Sonnet quaint.

There many a worthy Wight I've seen
In Ribbon blue and Ribbon green.
As *Oxford*, who a Wand doth bear,
Like *Moses*, in our Bibles fair;
Who for our Traffick forms Designs,
And gives to *Britain Indian* Mines.
Now, Shepherds, clip your fleecy Care,
Ye Maids, your Spinning-Wheels prepare,
Ye Weavers, all your Shuttles throw,
And bid broad Cloths and Serges grow,

For

PROLOGUE.

For Trading free fhall thrive again,
Nor Leafings leud affright the Swain.

There faw I *St. John*, fweet of Mien,
Full ftedfaft both to Church and Queen.
With whofe fair Name I'll deck my Strain,
St. John, right courteous to the Swain;

For thus he told me on a Day,
Trim are thy Sonnets, gentle *Gay*,
And certes, Mirth it were to fee
Thy joyous Madrigals twice three,
With Preface meet, and Notes profound,
Imprinted fair, and well y-bound.
All fuddenly then Home I fped,
And did ev'n as my Lord had faid.

Lo here, thou haft mine Eclogues fair,
But let not thefe detain thine Ear.

I et

PROLOGUE.

Let not th' Affairs of States and Kings
Wait, while our *Bowzybeus* sings.
Rather than Verse of simple Swain
Should stay the Trade of *France* or *Spain*,
Or for the Plaint of Parson's Maid,
Yon Emp'ror's Packets be delay'd;
In sooth, I swear by holy *Paul*,
I'd burn Book, Preface, Notes and all.

MON-

the Squabble.   Lud. Du Guernier inv. et Sculp.

MONDAY;

OR, THE

SQUABBLE.

Lobbin Clout, Cuddy, Cloddipole.

LOBBIN CLOUT

T H Y Younglings, *Cuddy*, are but juſt
awake,

No Thruſtles ſhrill the Bramble-Buſh
forſake,

No chirping Lark the Welkin ſheen invokes,

No Damſel yet the ſwelling Udder ſtrokes;

O'er yonder Hill does ſcant the Dawn appear, 5

Then why does *Cuddy* leave his Cott, ſo rear?

Line

3. Welkin *the ſame as* Welken, *an old* Saxon *Word ſignifying* a Cloud
by Poetical Licence it is frequently taken for the Element *or* Sky,
as may appear by this Verſe in the Dream *of* Chaucer. Ne in
all the Welkin was no Cloud.

Sheen *or* Shine, *an old Word for* ſhining *or* bright.

5. Scant, *uſed in ancient* British *Authors for* ſcarce.

6. Rear, *an Expreſſion in ſeveral Counties of* England, *for* early in
the Morning.

C U D D Y.

Ah *Lobbin Clout*! I ween, my Plight is gueſt,
For *he that loves, a Stranger is to Reſt*;
If Swains belye not, thou haſt prov'd the Smart,
And *Blouzelinda*'s Miſtreſs of thy Heart.　　　　10
This riſing rear betokeneth well thy Mind,
Thoſe Arms are folded for thy *Blouzelind.*
And well, I trow, our piteous Plights agree,
Thee *Blouzelinda* ſmites, *Buxoma* me.

L O B B I N   C L O U T.

Ah *Blouzelind*! I love thee more by half,　　15
Than Does their Fawns, or Cows the new-fall'n Calf:
Woe worth the Tongue! may Bliſters ſore it gall,
That names *Buxoma*, *Blouzelind* withal.

C U D D Y.

Hold, witleſs *Lobbin Clout*, I thee adviſe,
Leſt Bliſters ſore on thy own Tongue ariſe.　　20
Lo yonder *Cloddipole*, the blithſome Swain,
The wiſeſt Lout of all the neighbouring Plain.
From *Cloddipole* we learnt to read the Skies,
To know when Hail will fall, or Winds ariſe.

Line 7. To ween, *derived from the* Saxon, *to* think *or* conceive.

He

He taught us erſt the Heifers Tails to view, 25

When ſtuck aloft, that Show'rs would ſtrait enſue;

He firſt that uſeful Secret did explain,

That pricking Corns foretold the gath'ring Rain.

When Swallows fleet ſoar high and ſport in Air,

He told us that the Welkin wou'd be clear. 30

Let *Cloddipole* then hear us twain rehearſe,

And praiſe his Sweetheart in alternate Verſe.

I'll wager this ſame *Oaken Staff* with thee,

That *Cloddipole* ſhall give the Prize to me.

L O B B I N   C L O U T.

See this *Tobacco Pouch* that's lin'd with Hair, 35

Made of the Skin of ſleekeſt fallow Deer.

This Pouch, that's ty'd with Tape of reddeſt Hue,

I'll wager, that the Prize ſhall be my due.

C U D D Y.

Begin thy Carrols then, thou vaunting Slouch,

Be thine the *Oaken Staff*, or mine the *Pouch*. 40

L O B B I N   C L O U T.

My *Blouzelinda* is the blitheſt Laſs,

Than Primroſe ſweeter, or the Clover-Graſs.

Line

25. Erſt, *a Contraction of* ere this. *it ſignifies* ſometime ago *or* formerly.

Fair

Fair is the King-Cup that in Meadow blows,
Fair is the Daifie that befide her grows,
Fair is the Gillyflow'r, of Gardens fweet,   45
Fair is the Mary-Gold, for Pottage meet.
But *Blouzelind*'s than Gillyflow'r more fair,
Than Daifie, Mary-Gold, or King-Cup rare.

C U D D Y.

My brown *Buxoma* is the feateft Maid,
That e'er at Wake delightfome Gambol play'd. 50
Clean as young Lambkins or the Goofe's Down,
And like the Goldfinch in her *Sunday* Gown.
The witlefs Lambs may fport upon the Plain,
The frisking Kid delight the gaping Swain,
The wanton Calf may skip with many a Bound, 55
And my Cur *Tray* play defteft Feats around,
But neither Lamb nor Kid, nor Calf nor *Tray*,
Dance like *Buxoma* on the firft of *May*.

L O B B I N C L O U T.

Sweet is my Toil when *Blouzelind* is near,
Of her bereft 'tis Winter all the Year.   60
With her no fultry Summer's Heat I know;
In Winter, when fhe's nigh, with Love I glow.

Line 56. Deft, *an old Word fignifying* brisk *or* nimble.

Come *Blouzelinda*, eafe thy Swain's Defire,

My Summer's Shadow and my Winter's Fire!

C U D D Y.

As with *Buxoma* once I work'd at Hay,   65

Ev'n Noon-tide Labour feem'd an Holiday;

And Holidays, if haply fhe were gone,

Like Worky-days I wifh'd would foon be done.

Eftfoons, O Sweet-heart kind, my Love repay,

And all the Year fhall then be Holiday.   70

L O B B I N C L O U T.

As *Blouzelinda* in a gamefome Mood,

Behind a Haycock loudly laughing ftood,

I flily ran, and fnatch'd a hafty Kifs,

She wip'd her Lips, nor took it much amifs.

Believe me, *Cuddy*, while I'm bold to fay,   75

Her Breath was fweeter than the ripen'd Hay.

C U D D Y.

As my *Buxoma* in a Morning fair,

With gentle Finger ftroak'd her milky Care,

Line

69. Eftfoons. *from* eft *an ancient* Britifh *Word fignifying* foon. *So that* eft-
foons *is a doubling of the Word* foon, *which is, as it were to fay*
twice foon, *or very* foon.

I queintly ſtole a Kiſs; at firſt, 'tis true
She frown'd, yet after granted one or two.   80
Lobbin, I ſwear, believe who will my Vows,
Her Breath by far excell'd the breathing Cows.

LOBBIN CLOUT.

Leek to the *Welch,* to *Dutchmen Butter*'s dear,
Of *Iriſh* Swains *Potatoe* is the Chear;
Oats for their Feaſts the *Scottiſh* Shepherds grind,
Sweet *Turnips* are the Food of *Blouzelind.*   86
While ſhe loves *Turnips, Butter* I'll deſpiſe,
Nor *Leeks* nor *Oatmeal* nor *Potatoe* prize.

CUDDY.

In good *Roaſt Beef* my Landlord ſticks his Knife,
The *Capon* fat delights his dainty Wife,   90
Pudding our Parſon eats, the Squire loves *Hare,*
But *White-pot* thick is my *Buxoma*'s Fare.

Line

79. Queint *has various Significations in the ancient* Engliſh *Authors. I have uſed it in this Place in the ſame Senſe as* Chaucer *hath done in his* Miller's Tale. As Clerkes been full ſubtil and queint, *(by which he means* Arch *or* Waggiſh) *and not in that obſcene Senſe wherein he uſeth it in the Line immediately following.*

83. *Populus Alcidæ gratiſſima, vitis Iaccho,*
Formoſæ Myrtus Veneri, ſua Laurea Phœbo.
Phillis amat Corylos. Illas dum Phillis amabit,
Nec Myrtus vincet Corylos nec Laurea Phœbi. &c.   Virg.

While

While she loves *White-pot*, *Capon* ne'er shall be,
Nor *Hare*, nor *Beef*, nor *Pudding*, Food for me.

L O B B I N   C L O U T.

As once I play'd at *Blindman's-buff*, it hapt   95
About my Eyes the Towel thick was wrapt.
I miss'd the Swains, and seiz'd on *Blouzelind*;
True speaks that ancient Proverb, *Love is blind.*

C U D D Y.

As at *Hot-Cockles* once I laid me down,
And felt the weighty Hand of many a Clown; 100
Buxoma gave a gentle Tap, and I
Quick rose, and read soft Mischief in her Eye.

L O B B I N   C L O U T.

This Riddle, *Cuddy*, if thou canst, explain,
This wily Riddle puzzles ev'ry Swain.
† *What Flower is that which bears the* Virgin's *Name,*
The richest Metal joined with the same?   106

C U D D Y.

Answer, thou Carle, and judge this Riddle right,
I'll frankly own thee for a cunning Wight.
* *What Flow'r is that which Royal Honour craves,*
Adjoin the Virgin, *and 'tis strown on Graves.*   110

Line 109. *Dic quibus in terris inscripti nomina Regum*
          Nascantur Flores. Virg.   † *Marygold.* * *Rosemary.*

CLODDIPOLE.

Forbear, contending Louts, give o'er your Strains,
An *Oaken Staff* each merits for his Pains.
But fee the Sun-Beams bright to Labour warn,
And gild the Thatch of Goodman *Hodges'* Barn.
Your Herds for want of Water ftand adry,   115
They're weary of your Songs——and fo am I.

Line 112. *Et vitula tu dignus & hic.* Virg.

the Ditty   Lud. Du Guernier inv. et sculp.

TUESDAY;

OR, THE

DITTY.

MARIAN.

OUNG *Colin Clout*, a Lad of peer-
     less Meed,
     Full well could dance, and deftly tune
     the Reed;
In ev'ry Wood his Carrols sweet were known,
In ev'ry Wake his nimble Feats were shown.
When in the Ring the Rustick Routs he threw, 5
The Damsels Pleasures with his Conquests grew;
Or when aslant the Cudgel threats his Head,
His Danger smites the Breast of ev'ry Maid,
But chief of *Marian*. *Marian* lov'd the Swain,
The Parson's Maid, and neatest of the Plain. 10
Marian that soft could stroak the udder'd Cow,
Or with her Winnow ease the Barly Mow;

Marbled

Marbled with Sage the hard'ning Cheese she press'd,
And yellow Butter *Marian's* Skill confess'd;
But *Marian* now devoid of Country Cares,   15
Nor yellow Butter nor Sage Cheese prepares.
For yearning Love the witless Maid employs,
And *Love,* say Swains, *all busie Heed destroys.*
Colin makes mock at all her piteous Smart,
A Lass that *Cic'ly* hight, had won his Heart,   20
Cic'ly the Western Lass that tends the *Kee,*
The Rival of the Parson's Maid was she.
In dreary Shade now *Marian* lyes along,
And mixt with Sighs thus wails in plaining Song.

    Ah woful Day! ah woful Noon and Morn!   25
When first by thee my Younglings white were shorn,
Then first, I ween, I cast a Lover's Eye,
My Sheep were silly, but more silly I.
Beneath the Shears they felt no lasting Smart,
They lost but Fleeces while I lost a Heart.   30

Line 21. Kee, *a West-Country Word for* Kine *or* Cows.

Ah

Ah *Colin*! canſt thou leave thy Sweetheart true!
What I have done for thee will *Cic'ly* do?
Will ſhe thy Linnen waſh or Hoſen darn,
And knit thee Gloves made of her own-ſpun Yarn?
Will ſhe with Huſwife's Hand provide thy Meat,
And ev'ry *Sunday* Morn thy Neckcloth plait?   36
Which o'er thy Kerſey Doublet ſpreading wide,
In Service-Time drew *Cic'ly*'s Eyes aſide.

Where-e'er I gad I cannot hide my Care,
My new Diſaſters in my Look appear.   40
White as the Curd my ruddy Cheek is grown,
So thin my Features that I'm hardly known;
Our Neighbours tell me oft in joking Talk
Of Aſhes, Leather, Oatmeal, Bran and Chalk;
Unwittingly of *Marian* they divine,   45
And wiſt not that with thoughtful Love I pine.
Yet *Colin Clout*, untoward Shepherd Swain,
Walks whiſtling blithe, while pitiful I plain.

Whilom with thee 'twas *Marian*'s dear Delight
To moil all Day, and merry make at Night.   50

If

If in the Soil you guide the crooked Share,

Your early Breakfaſt is my conſtant Care.

And when with even Hand you ſtrow the Grain,

I fright the thieviſh Rookes from off the Plain.

In miſling Days when I my Threſher heard,   55

With nappy Beer I to the Barn repair'd;

Loſt in the Muſick of the whirling Flail,

To gaze on thee I left the ſmoaking Pail;

In Harveſt when the Sun was mounted high,

My Leathern Bottle did thy Drought ſupply; 60

When-e'er you mow'd I follow'd with the Rake,

And have full oft been Sun-burnt for thy Sake;

When in the Welkin gath'ring Show'rs were ſeen,

I lagg'd the laſt with *Colin* on the Green;

And when at Eve returning with thy Carr,   65

Awaiting heard the gingling Bells from far;

Strait on the Fire the ſooty Pot I plac't,

To warm thy Broth I burnt my Hands for Haſte.

When hungry thou ſtood'ſt *ſtaring, like an Oaf*,

I ſlic'd the Luncheon from the Barly Loaf, 70

With crumbled Bread I thicken'd well thy Meſs.

Ah, love me more, or love thy Pottage leſs!

Laſt

Laſt *Friday*'s Eve, when as the Sun was ſet,
I, near yon Stile, three ſallow Gypſies met.
Upon my Hand they caſt a poring Look,   75
Bid me beware, and thrice their Heads they ſhook,
They ſaid that many Croſſes I muſt prove,
Some in my worldly Gain, but moſt in Love.
Next Morn I miſs'd three Hens and our old Cock,
And off the Hedge two Pinners and a Smock. 80
I bore theſe Loſſes with a Chriſtian Mind,
And no Miſhaps could feel, while thou wert kind.
But ſince, alas! I grew my *Colin*'s Scorn,
I've known no Pleaſure, Night, or Noon, or Morn.
Help me, ye Gipſies, bring him home again,   85
And to a conſtant Laſs give back her Swain.

Have I not ſate with thee full many a Night,
When dying Embers were our only Light,
When ev'ry Creature did in Slumbers lye,
Beſides our Cat, my *Colin Clout*, and I?   90
No troublous Thoughts the Cat or *Colin* move,
While I alone am kept awake by Love.

Remember, *Colin,* when at laſt Year's Wake,
I bought the coſtly Preſent for thy ſake,   94
Couldſt thou ſpell o'er the Poſie on thy Knife,
And with another change thy State of Life?
If thou forget'ſt, I wot, I can repeat,
My Memory can tell the Verſe ſo ſweet.
As this is grav'd upon this Knife of thine,
So is thy Image on this Heart of mine.   100
But Woe is me! Such Preſents luckleſs prove,
For *Knives,* they tell me, *always ſever Love.*

Thus *Marian* wail'd, her Eye with Tears brimfull,
When Goody *Dobbins* brought her Cow to Bull.
With Apron blue to dry her Tears ſhe ſought, 105
Then ſaw the Cow well ſerv'd, and took a Groat.

WED·

the Dumps.   Lud. Du Guernier inv et sculp.

WEDNESDAY;

OR, THE

**D U M P S.*

SPARABELLA.

HE Wailings of a Maiden I recite,
A Maiden fair, that *Sparabella* hight.
Such Strains ne'er warble in the Lin-
nets Throat,

Nor the gay Goldfinch chaunts so sweet a Note,

No Mag-pye chatter'd, nor the painted Jay,　　5

Nor Ox was heard to low, nor Ass to bray.

*Dumps, or Dumbs, made use of to express a Fit of the Sullens. Some have pretended that it is derived from Dumops a King of Egypt, that built a Pyramid, and dy'd of Melancholy. So Mopes after the same Manner is thought to have come from Merops, another Egyptian King that dy'd of the same Distemper; but our English Antiquaries have conjectured that Dumps, which is, a grievous Heaviness of Spirits, comes from the Word Dumplin, the heaviest kind of Pudding that is eaten in this Country, much used in Norfolk, and other Counties of England.

Line

*5. Immemor Herbarum quos est mirata juvenca
Certantes quorum stupefacta carmine Lynces;
Et mutata suos requierunt flumina cursus. Virg.*

No ruſling Breezes play'd the Leaves among,
While thus her Madrigal the Damſel ſung.

A while, O *D——y*, lend an Ear or twain,
Nor, though in homely Guiſe, my Verſe diſdain; 10
Whether thou ſeek'ſt new Kingdoms in the Sun,
Whether thy Muſe does at *New-Market* run,
Or does with Goſſips at a Feaſt regale,
And heighten her Conceits with Sack and Ale,
Or elſe at Wakes with *Joan* and *Hodge* rejoice, 15
Where *D——y*'s Lyricks ſwell in every Voice;
Yet ſuffer me, thou Bard of wond'rous Meed,
Amid thy Bays to weave this rural Weed.

Now the Sun drove adown the weſtern Road,
And Oxen laid at reſt forget the Goad,　　　　20

Line

9. *Tu mihi ſeu magni ſuperas jam ſaxa Timavi,*
   Sive oram Illyrici legis æquoris——

11. *An Opera written by this Author, called the* World in the Sun, *or the* Kingdom of Birds; *he is alſo famous for his Song on the* New-market Horſe Race, *and ſeveral others that are ſung by the* Britiſh Swains.

17 Meed, *an old Word for* Fame *or* Renown.

18. —— *Hanc ſine tempora circum*
    Inter Victrices ederam tibi ſerpere lauros.

The

The Clown fatigu'd trudg'd homeward with his
[Spade,
Across theMeadows stretch'd the lengthen'd Shade;
When *Sparabella* pensive and forlorn,
Alike with yearning Love and Labour worn,
Lean'd on her Rake, and strait with doleful Guise 25
Did this sad Plaint in moanful Notes devise.

Come Night as dark as Pitch, surround my Head,
From *Sparabella Bumkinet* is fled;
The Ribbon that his val'rous Cudgel won,
Last *Sunday* happier *Clumsilis* put on.   30
Sure, if he'd Eyes (*but Love, they say, has none*)
I whilome by that Ribbon had been known.
Ah, Well-a-day! I'm shent with baneful Smart,
For with the Ribbon he bestow'd his Heart.

My Plaint, ye Lasses, with this Burthen aid, 35
'Tis hard so true a Damsel dies a Maid.

Shall heavy *Clumsilis* with me compare?
View this, ye Lovers, and like me despair.

Line
25. *Incumbens tereti Damon sic cæpit Oliva.*
33. Shent, *an old Word signifying* Hurt *or* harmed.
37. *Mopso Nisa datur, quid non speremus Amantes?* Virg.
C 4
Her

Her blubber'd Lip by ſmutty Pipes is worn,

And in her Breath Tobacco Whiffs are born;   40

The cleanly Cheeſe-preſs ſhe could never turn,

Her awkward Fiſt did ne'er employ the Churn;

If e'er ſhe brew'd, the Drink wou'd ſtrait grow ſour,

Before it ever felt the Thunder's Pow'r:

No Huſwifry the dowdy Creature knew;   45

To ſum up all, her Tongue confeſs'd the Shrew.

My Plaint, ye Laſſes, with this Burthen aid,

'Tis hard ſo true a Damſel dies a Maid.

I've often ſeen my Viſage in yon Lake,

Nor are my Features of the homelieſt Make.   50

Though *Clumſilis* may boaſt a whiter Dye,

Yet the black Sloe turns in my rolling Eye;

And faireſt Bloſſoms drop with ev'ry Blaſt,

But the brown Beauty will like Hollies laſt.

Her wan Complexion's like the wither'd Leek,   55

While *Katherine* Pears adorn my ruddy Cheek.

Line
49. *Nec ſum adeo informis, nuper me in Littore vidi.* Virg.
53. *Alba liguſtra cadunt, vaccinia nigra leguntur.* Virg.

Yet

Yet she, alas! the witless Lout hath won,

And by her Gain, poor *Sparabell*'s undone!

Let Hares and Hounds in coupling Straps unite,

The clocking Hen make Friendship with the Kite,

Let the Fox simply wear the Nuptial Noose, 61

And join in Wedlock with the wadling Goose;

For Love hath brought a stranger thing to pass,

The fairest Shepherd weds the foulest Lass.

My Plaint, ye Lasses, with this Burthen aid, 65
'Tis hard so true a Damsel dies a Maid.

Sooner shall Cats disport in Waters clear,

And speckled Mackrel graze the Meadows fair,

Sooner shall scriech Owls bask in Sunny Day,

And the slow Ass on Trees, like Squirrels, play, 70

Sooner shall Snails on insect Pinions rove,

Than I forget my Shepherd's wonted Love!

My Plaint, ye Lasses, with this Burthen aid,
'Tis hard so true a Damsel dies a Maid.

Line
59. *Jungentur jam Gryphes equis; avoque sequenti*
 Cum canibus timidi venient ad pocula Damæ. Virg.
67. *Ante leves ergo pascentur in æthere Cervi*
 Et freta destituent nudos in littore Pisces ——
 Quam nostro illius labatur pectore vultus. Virg.

Ah!

Ah! didſt thou know what Proffers I withſtood,

When late I met the *Squire* in yonder Wood! 76

To me he ſped, regardleſs of his Game,

Whilſt all my Cheek was glowing red with Shame;

My Lip he kiſs'd, and prais'd my healthful Look,

Then from his Purſe of Silk a *Guinea* took, 80

Into my Hand he forc'd the tempting Gold,

While I with modeſt ſtruggling broke his Hold.

He ſwore that *Dick* in Liv'ry ſtrip'd with Lace,

Should wed me ſoon to keep me from Diſgrace;

But I nor Footman priz'd nor golden Fee, 85

For what is Lace or Gold compar'd to thee?

My Plaint, ye Laſſes, with this Burthen aid,

'Tis hard ſo true a Damſel dies a Maid.

Now plain I ken whence *Love* his Riſe begun

Sure he was born ſome bloody *Butcher's* Son, 90

Line

89. To ken. *Scire.* Chaucero, *to Ken;* and Kende *notus A. S.* cunnan *Goth.* Kunnan. *Germanis* Kennen, *Danis* Kiende. *Iſlandis* Kunna. *Belgis* Kennen. *This Word is of general uſe, but not very common, though not unknown to the Vulgar.* Ken *for* proſpicere *is well known and uſed to diſcover by the Eye.* Ray. F. R. S.

Nunc ſcio quid ſit Amor, &c.

Crudelis mater magis an puer improbus ille?

Improbus ille puer, crudelis tu queque mater. Virg.

Bred

Bred up in Shambles, where our Younglings flain,

Erſt taught him Miſchief and to ſport with Pain.

The *Father* only filly Sheep annoys,

The *Son,* the fillier Shepherdeſs deſtroys.

Does *Son* or *Father* greater Miſchief do? 95

The *Sire* is cruel, ſo the *Son* is too.

My Plaint, ye Laſſes, with this Burthen aid,

'Tis hard ſo true a Damſel dies a Maid.

[flow;

Farewel, ye Woods, ye Meads, ye Streams that

A ſudden Death ſhall rid me of my Woe. 100

This Penknife keen my Windpipe ſhall divide.———

What, ſhall I fall as ſqueaking Pigs have dy'd!

No——To ſome Tree this Carcaſs I'll ſuſpend. ——

But worrying Curs find ſuch untimely End!

I'll ſpeed me to the Pond, where the high Stool 105

On the long Plank hangs o'er the muddy Pool,

That Stool, the dread of ev'ry ſcolding Quean. ——

Yet, ſure a Lover ſhould not dye ſo mean!

Line

99. ——— ——— ——— *vivite Sylvæ,*
Præceps aerii ſpecula de montis in undas
Deferar. Virg.

There plac'd aloft, I'll rave and rail by Fits,
Though all the Parish say I've loft my Wits; 110
And thence, if Courage holds, my felf I'll throw,
And quench my Paffion in the Lake below.

Ye Laffes, ceafe your Burthen, ceafe to moan,
And, by my Cafe forewarn'd, go mind your own.

The Sun was fet; the Night came on a-pace,
And falling Dews bewet around the Place, 116
The Bat takes airy Rounds on leathern Wings,
And the hoarfe Owl his woeful Dirges fings;
The prudent Maiden deems it now too late,
And 'till to Morrow comes, defers her Fáte. 120

THURSDAY;

the Spell. Lud. Du Guernier inv. et sculp.

THURSDAY;

OR, THE

SPELL.

HOBNELIA.

OBNELIA seated in a dreary Vale,

In pensive Mood rehears'd her piteous
Tale,

Her piteous Tale the Winds in Sighs
bemoan,

And pining Eccho answers Groan for Groan.

I rue the Day, a rueful Day I trow,   5

The woful Day, a Day indeed of Woe!

When *Lubberkin* to Town his Cattle drove,

A Maiden fine bedight he hapt to love;

Line.
8. Dight *or* bedight, *from the* Saxon *Word* Dihtan, *which signifies to
set in order.*

The

The Maiden fine bedight his Love retains,
And for the Village he forsakes the Plains.   10
Return, my *Lubberkin*, these Ditties hear ;
Spells will I try, and Spells shall ease my Care.

    With my sharp Heel I three times mark the Ground,
And turn me thrice around, around, around.

    When first the Year, I heard the Cuckow sing, 15
And call with welcome Note the budding Spring,
I straitway set a running with such Haste,
Deb'rah that won the Smock scarce ran so fast.
'Till spent for lack of Breath, quite weary grown,
Upon a rising Bank I sat adown,   20
Then doff'd my Shoe, and by my Troth, I swear,
Therein I spy'd this yellow frizled Hair,
As like to *Lubberkin*'s in Curl and Hue,
As if upon his comely Pate it grew.

    With my sharp Heel I three times mark the Ground,
And turn me thrice around, around, around.

Line
21. Doff *and* Don, *contracted from the Words* do off *and* do on.

At

At Eve laſt *Midſummer* no Sleep I ſought,
But to the Field a Bag of Hemp-ſeed brought,
I ſcatter'd round the Seed on ev'ry ſide,
And three times in a trembling Accent cry'd.   30
This Hempſeed with my Virgin Hands I ſow,
Who ſhall my True-love be, the Crop ſhall mow.
I ſtrait look'd back, and if my Eyes ſpeak Truth,
With his keen Scythe behind me came the Youth.
  With my ſharp Heel I three times mark the Ground,
And turn me thrice around, around, around.   36

  Laſt *Valentine,* the Day when Birds of Kind
Their Paramours with mutual Chirpings find;
I rearly roſe, juſt at the break of Day,
Before the Sun had chas'd the Stars away;   40
A-field I went, amid the Morning Dew
To milk my Kine (for ſo ſhould Huſwives do)
Thee firſt I ſpy'd, and the firſt Swain we ſee,
In ſpite of Fortune ſhall our True-love be;
See, *Lubberkin,* each Bird his Partner take,   45
And can'ſt thou then thy Sweetheart dear forſake?

With

With my sharp Heel I three times mark the Ground,
And turn me thrice around, around, around.

Last *May-day* fair I search'd to find a Snail
That might my secret Lover's Name reveal;   50
Upon a Gooseberry Bush a Snail I found,
For always Snails near sweetest Fruit abouna.
I seiz'd the Vermine, home I quickly sped,
And on the Hearth the milk-white Embers spread.
Slow crawl'd the Snail, and if I right can spell, 55
In the soft Ashes mark'd a curious *L*:
Oh, may this wondrous Omen lucky prove!
For *L* is found in *Lubberkin* and *Love.*

With my sharp Heel I three times mark the Ground,
And turn me thrice around, around, around.   60

Two Hazel-Nuts I threw into the Flame.
And to each Nut I gave a Sweet-heart's Name.
This with the loudest Bounce me sore amaz'd,
That in a Flame of brightest Colour blaz'd.

Line
64.———ἐγὼ δ᾽ ὁπὶ Δέλφιδι δάφναν
Αἴθω. χ᾽ ὡς αὐτὰ λακέει μέγα καππυρίσασα.   Theoc.

As

As blaz'd the Nut so may thy Paſſion grow, 65
For 'twas *thy Nut* that did so brightly glow.

 With my ſharp Heel I three times mark the Ground,
And turn me thrice around, around, around.

 As Peaſcods once I pluck'd, I chanc'd to ſee
One that was cloſely fill'd with three times three,
Which when I crop'd I ſafely home convey'd, 71
And o'er my Door the Spell in ſecret laid.
My Wheel I turn'd, and ſung a Ballad new,
While from the Spindle I the Fleeces drew;
The Latch mov'd up, when who ſhould firſt come in,
But in his proper Perſon, —— *Lubberkin.* 76
I broke my Yarn ſurpriz'd the Sight to ſee,
Sure Sign that he would break his Word with me.
Eftſoons I join'd it with my wonted Slight,
So may again his Love with mine unite! 80

 With my ſharp Heel I three times mark the Ground,
And turn me thrice around, around, around.

 This *Lady-fly* I take from off the Graſs,
Whoſe ſpotted Back might ſcarlet Red ſurpaſs.

Line 66. *Daphnis me malus urit, ego hanc in Daphnide.*

   Fly,

Fly, Lady-Bird, *North, South, or Eaſt or Weſt*, 85
Fly where the Man is found that I love beſt.
He leaves my Hand, ſee to the *Weſt* he's flown,
To call my True-love from the faithleſs Town.

With my ſharp Heel I three times mark the Ground,
And turn me thrice around, around, around. 90

This mellow Pippin, which I pare around,
My Shepherd's Name ſhall flouriſh on the Ground.
I fling th'unbroken Paring o'er my Head,
Upon the Graſs a perfect L is read;
Yet on my Heart a fairer L is ſeen 95
Than what the Paring marks upon the Green.

With my ſharp Heel I three times mark the Ground,
And turn me thrice around, around, around.

This Pippin ſhall another Tryal make,
See from the Core two Kernels brown I take; 100
This on my Cheek for *Lubberkin* is worn,
And *Boobyclod* on t'other ſide is born.

Line
93. *Tranſque Caput jace; ne reſpexeris.* Virg.

But

But *Boobyclod* foon drops upon the Ground,
A certain Token that his Love's unfound,
While *Lubberkin* fticks firmly to the laft;   105
Oh were his Lips to mine but join'd fo faft!

With my fharp Heel I three times mark the Ground,
And turn me thrice around, around, around.

As *Lubberkin* once flept beneath a Tree,
I twitch'd his dangling Garter from his Knee;   110
He wift not when the hempen String I drew,
Now mine I quickly doff of Inkle Blue;
Together faft I tye the Garters twain,
And while I knit the Knot repeat this Strain.
Three times a True-love's Knot I tye fecure,   115
Firm be the Knot, firm may his Love endure.

With my fharp Heel I three times mark the Ground,
And turn me thrice around, around, around.

As I was wont, I trudg'd laft Market-Day   119
To Town, with New-laid Eggs preferv'd in Hay.

Line
109. *Necte tribus nodis ternos, Amarylli, Colores*
  Necte, Amarylli modo; & Veneris dic vincula necto. Virg.

D 3   1

I made my Market long before 'twas Night,

My Purfe grew heavy and my Basket light.

Strait to the Pothecary's Shop I went,

And in Love-Powder all my Mony spent;

Behap what will, next Sunday after Prayers,   125

When to the Ale-house *Lubberkin* repairs,

These *Golden Flies* into his Mug I'll throw,

And soon the Swain with fervent Love shall glow.

With my sharp Heel I three times mark the Ground,

And turn me thrice around, around, around.   130

[Ears,

But hold —— our *Light-Foot* barks, and cocks his

O'er yonder Stile see *Lubberkin* appears.

He comes, he comes, *Hobnelia*'s not bewray'd,

Nor shall she crown'd with Willow die a Maid.

He vows, he swears, he'll give me a green Gown,

Oh dear! I fall *adown, adown, adown!*   136

Line

123. *Has Herbas, atque hæc Ponto mihi lecta venena,*
     Ipse dedit Maris.   Virg.

127 ————————Ποτὸν κακὸν ἄυεἰον ὀισῶ.   Theoc.

131. *Nescio quid certe est: & Hylax in limine latrat.*

FRIDAY;

the Dirge Lud DuGuernier inv & Sculp

FRIDAY;

OR, THE

*DIRGE.

BUMKINET. GRUBBINOL.

BUMKINET.

HY, *Grubbinol,* doft thou fo wiftful
  feem?

There's Sorrow in thy Look, if right
  I deem.

'Tis true, yon Oaks with yellow Tops appear,

And chilly Blafts begin to nip the Year;

---

* Dirge, or Dyrge, *a mournful Ditty, or Song of Lamentation over the
  dead, not a Contraction of the Latin Dirige' in the Popish Hymn* Diri-
  ge Greffus meos, *as some pretend. But from the Teutonick* Dyrke,
  Laudare, *to praise and extol. Whence it is possible their* Dyrke *and
  our* Dirge, *was a laudatory Song to commemorate and applaud the
  Dead.* Cowell's Interpreter.

From

From the tall Elm a Show'r of Leaves is born,   5

And their loft Beauty riven Beeches mourn.

Yet ev'n this Seafon Pleafance blithe affords,

Now the fqueez'd Prefs foams with our Apple Hoards.

Come, let us hye, and quaff a cheery Bowl,

Let Cyder New *wafh Sorrow from thy Soul.*   10

GRUBBINOL.

Ah *Bumkinet*! fince thou from hence wert gone,

From thefe fad Plains all Merriment is flown;

Should I reveal my Grief 'twould fpoil thy Chear,

And make thine Eye o'erflow with many a Tear.

BUMKINET.

Hang Sorrow! Let's to yonder Hutt repair,   15

And with trim Sonnets *caft away our Care.*

Gillian of Croydon well thy Pipe can play,

Thou fing'ft moft fweet, *o'er Hills and far away.*

Of *Patient Griffel* I devife to fing,

And Catches quaint fhall make the Vallies ring. 20

Come, *Grubbinol*, beneath this Shelter, come,

From hence we view our Flocks fecurely roam.

Line

15. *Incipe Mopfe prior fi quos aut Phyllidis ignes*
    Aut Alconis habes Laudes, aut jurgia Codri.

GRUB-

G R U B B I N O L.

Yes, blithesome Lad, a Tale I mean to sing,
But with my Woe shall distant Valleys ring.
The Tale shall make our Kidlings droop their Head,
For Woe is me!---our *Blouzelind* is dead.   26

B U M K I N E T.

Is *Blouzelinda* dead? farewel my Glee!
No Happiness is now reserv'd for me.
As the Wood Pidgeon cooes without his Mate,
So shall my doleful Dirge bewail her Fate.   30
Of *Blouzelinda* fair I mean to tell,
The peerless Maid that did all Maids excell.

Henceforth the Morn shall dewy Sorrow shed,
And Ev'ning Tears upon the Grass be spread;
The rolling Streams with watry Grief shall flow, 35
And Winds shall moan aloud---when loud they blow.
Henceforth, as oft as *Autumn* shall return,
The dropping Trees, whene'er it rains, shall mourn;
This Season quite shall strip the Country's Pride,
For 'twas in *Autumn Blouzelinda* dy'd.   40

27. Glee, *Joy. from the* Dutch, Glooren, *to* recreate.

Where-e'er

Where-e'er I gad, I *Blouzelind* fhall view,
Woods, Dairy, Barn and Mows our Paffion knew.
When I direct my Eyes to yonder Wood,
Frefh rifing Sorrow curdles in my Blood.
Thither I've often been the Damfel's Guide,   45
When rotten Sticks our Fuel have fupply'd;
There, I remember how her Faggots large,
Were frequently thefe happy Shoulders charge.
Sometimes this Crook drew Hazel Boughs adown,
And ftuff'd her Apron wide with Nuts fo brown;
Or when her feeding Hogs had mifs'd their Way, 51
Or wallowing 'mid a Feaft of Acorns lay;
Th' untoward Creatures to the Stye I drove,
And whiftled all the Way---or told my Love.

If by the Dairy's Hatch I chance to hie,   55
I fhall her goodly Countenance efpie,
For there her goodly Countenance I've feen,
Set off with Kerchief ftarch'd and Pinners clean.
Sometimes, like Wax, fhe rolls the Butter round,
Or with the wooden Lilly prints the Pound.   60

Whilome

Whilome I've feen her skim the clouted Cream,
And prefs from fpongy Curds the milky Stream.
But now, alas! thefe Ears fhall hear no more
The whining Swine furround the Dairy Door,
No more her Care fhall fill the hollow Tray, 65
To fat the guzzling Hogs with Floods of Whey.
Lament, ye Swine, in Gruntings fpend your Grief,
For you, like me, have loft your fole Relief.

When in the Barn the founding Flail I ply,
Where from her Sieve the Chaff was wont to fly,
The Poultry there will feem around to ftand, 71
Waiting upon her charitable Hand.
No Succour meet the Poultry now can find,
For they, like me, have loft their *Blouzelind*.

Whenever by yon Barley Mow I pafs, 75
Before my Eyes will trip the tidy Lafs.
I pitch'd the Sheaves (oh could I do fo now)
Which fhe in Rows pil'd on the growing Mow.
There ev'ry deale my Heart by Love was gain'd,
There the fwect Kifs my Courtfhip has explain'd.

Ah

Ah *Blouzelind*! that Mow I ne'er shall see,   81
But thy Memorial will revive in me.

Lament, ye Fields, and rueful Symptoms show,
Henceforth let not the smelling Primrose grow;
Let Weeds instead of Butter-flow'rs appear,   85
And Meads, instead of Daisies, Hemlock bear;
For Cowslips sweet let Dandelions spread,
For *Blouzelinda*, blithsome Maid, is dead!
Lament ye Swains, and o'er her Grave bemoan,
And spell ye right this Verse upon her Stone.   90
Here Blouzelinda *lyes*——*Alas*, *alas*!
Weep Shepherds.——*and remember Flesh is Grass.*

GRUBBINOL.

Albeit thy Songs are sweeter to mine Ear,
Than to the thirsty Cattle Rivers clear;

Line
84. *Pro molli violâ, pro purpureo Narcisso*
    Carduus, & spinis surgit Paliurus acutis.   Virg.
90. *Et Tumulum facite, & tumulo superaddite Carmen.*
93. *Tale tuum Carmen nobis, Divine Poeta,*
    Quale sopor fessis in gramine: quale per æstum
    Dulcis aquæ saliente sitim restinguere rivo.
    Nos tamen hæc quocumque modo tibi nostra vicissim
    Dicemus, Daphninque tuum tollemus ad astra.   Virg.

Or

Or Winter Porridge to the lab'ring Youth,   95
Or Bunns and Sugar to the Damfel's Tooth;
Yet *Blouzelinda*'s Name fhall tune my Lay,
Of her I'll fing for ever and for aye.

When *Blouzelind* expir'd, the Weather's Bell
Before the drooping Flock toll'd forth her Knell;
The folemn Death-watch click'd the Hour fhe dy'd,
And fhrilling Crickets in the Chimney cry'd;
The boding Raven on her Cottage fate,
And with hoarfe Croaking warn'd us of her Fate;
The Lambkin, which her wonted Tendance bred,
Drop'd on the Plains that fatal Inftant dead;   106
Swarm'd on a rotten Stick the Bees I fpy'd,
Which erft I faw when Goody *Dobfon* dy'd.

How fhall I, void of Tears, her Death relate,
While on her Dearling's Bed her Mother fate!   110
Thefe Words the dying *Blouzelinda* fpoke,
And *of the Dead let none the Will revoke.*

Line
Κρέασον μελπομενω τευ ακυέμεν ἢ μέγι λῶχεν.   Theoc.

Mother,

Mother, quoth she, let not the Poultry need,

And give the Goose wherewith to raise her Breed,

Be these my Sister's Care----and ev'ry Morn 115

Amid the Ducklings let her scatter Corn;

The sickly Calf that's hous'd, be sure to tend,

Feed him with Milk, and from bleak Colds defend.

Yet e'er I die----see, Mother, yonder Shelf,

There secretly I've hid my worldly Pelf. 120

Twenty good Shillings in a Rag I laid,

Be ten the Parson's, for my Sermon paid.

The rest is yours---My Spinning-Wheel and Rake,

Let *Susan* keep for her dear Sister's sake;

My new Straw Hat that's trimly lin'd with Green,

Let *Peggy* wear, for she's a Damsel clean. 126

My leathern Bottle, long in Harvests try'd,

Be *Grubbinol's*---this Silver Ring beside:

Three silver Pennies, and a Ninepence bent,

A Token kind, to *Bumkinet* is sent. 130

Thus spoke the Maiden, while her Mother cry'd,

And peaceful, like the harmless Lamb, she dy'd.

To

To fhow their Love, the Neighbours far and near,
Follow'd with wiftful Look the Damfel's Bier.
Sprigg'd Rofemary the Lads and Laffes bore,   135
While difmally the Parfon walk'd before.
Upon her Grave their Rofemary they threw,
The Daifie, Butter-flow'r and Endive Blue.

After the good Man warn'd us from his Text,
That None could tell whofe Turn would be the next;
He faid, that Heav'n would take her Soul no doubt.
And fpoke the Hour-glafs in her Praife---quite out.

To her fweet Mem'ry flow'ry Garlands ftrung,
O'er her now empty Seat aloft were hung.   144
With wicker Rods we fenc'd her Tomb around,
To ward from Man and Beaft the hallow'd Ground,
Left her new Grave the Parfon's Cattle raze,
For both his Horfe and Cow the Church-yard graze.

Now we trudg'd homeward to her Mother's Farm,
To drink new Cyder mull'd, with Ginger warm.

For Gaffer *Tread-well* told us by the by,   151
Exceſſive Sorrow is exceeding dry.

While Bulls bear Horns upon their curled Brow,
Or Laſſes with ſoft Stroakings milk the Cow;
While padling Ducks the ſtanding Lake deſire,
Or batt'ning Hogs roll in the ſinking Mire;   156
While Moles the crumbled Earth in Hillocks raiſe,
So long ſhall Swains tell *Blouzelinda*'s Praiſe.

Thus wail'd the Louts, in melancholy Strain,
'Till bonny *Suſan* ſped a-croſs the Plain;   160
They ſeiz'd the Laſs in Apron clean array'd,
And to the Ale-houſe forc'd the willing Maid;
In Ale and Kiſſes they forget their Cares,
And *Suſan Blouzelinda*'s Loſs repairs.

Line

153 *Dum juga montis Aper, fluvios dum Piſcis amabit*
Dumque Thymo paſcentur apes, Dum rore cicadæ,
Semper honos nomenque tuum, laudeſque manebunt.   Virg.

the Flights.　　　　Lud. Du Guernier inv et sculp.

SATURDAY;

OR, THE

FLIGHTS.

BOWZYBEUS.

UBLIMER Strains, O ruſtick
  Muſe, prepare;
  Forget a-while the Barn and Dai-
  ry's Care;
Thy homely Voice to loftier Numbers raiſe,
The Drunkard's Flights require ſonorous Lays,
With *Bowzybeus*' Songs exalt thy Verſe,   5
While Rocks and Woods the various Notes rehearſe.

'Twas in the Seaſon when the Reaper's Toil
Of the ripe Harveſt 'gan to rid the Soil;

Wide through the Field was feen a goodly Rout,
Clean Damfels bound the gather'd Sheaves about, 10
The Lads with fharpen'd Hook and fweating Brow
Cut down the Labours of the Winter Plow.
To the near Hedge young *Sufan* fteps afide,
She feign'd her Coat or Garter was unty'd,
What-e'er fhe did, fhe ftoop'd adown unfeen, 15
And merry Reapers, what they lift, will ween.
Soon fhe rofe up, and cry'd with Voice fo fhrill
That Eccho anfwer'd from the diftant Hill;
The Youths and Damfels ran to *Sufan*'s Aid,
Who thought fome Adder had the Lafs difmay'd.

When faft afleep they *Bowzybeus* fpy'd, 21
His Hat and oaken Staff lay clofe befide.
That *Bowzybeus* who could fweetly fing,
Or with the rozin'd Bow torment the String;
That *Bowzybeus* who with Finger's fpeed 25
Could call foft Warblings from the breathing Reed;
That *Bowzybeus* who with jocond Tongue,
Ballads and Roundelays and Catches fung.

Line 22. *Serta procul tantum capiti delapfa jacebant.* Virg.

They

They loudly laugh to fee the Damfel's Fright,
And in difport furround the drunken Wight.   30

Ah *Bowzybeë*, why didft thou ftay fo long, [ftrong!
The Mugs were large, the Drink was wondrous
Thou fhould'ft have left the Fair before 'twas Night,
But thou fat'ft toping 'till the Morning Light.

Cic'ly, brisk Maid, fteps forth before the Rout, 35
And kifs'd with fmacking Lip the fnoring Lout.
For Cuftom fays, *Who-e'er this Venture proves,*
For fuch a Kifs demands a pair of Gloves.
By her Example *Dorcas* bolder grows,
And plays a tickling Straw within his Nofe.   40
He rubs his Noftril, and in wonted Joke

                                    [fpoke.
The fneering Swains with ftamm'ring Speech be-
To you, my Lads, I'll fing my Carrols o'er,
As for the Maids, ——I've fomething elfe in ftore.

Line
40. *Sanguineis frontem Moris & Tempora pingit.*   Virg.
43. *Carmina quæ vultis, cognofcite, carmina vobis.*
    Huic aliud Mercedis erit.   Virg.

E 4   No

No sooner 'gan he raise his tuneful Song,   45
But Lads and Lasses round about him throng.
Not Ballad-singer plac'd above the Croud
Sings with a Note so shrilling sweet and loud,
Nor Parish Clerk who calls the Psalm so clear,
Like *Bowzybeus* sooths th' attentive Ear.   50

Of Nature's Laws his Carrols first begun,
Why the grave Owl can never face the Sun.
For Owles, as Swains observe, detest the Light,
And only sing and seek their Prey by Night.
How Turnips hide their swelling Heads below,
And how the closing Colworts upwards grow;
How *Will-a-Wisp* mis-leads Night-faring Clowns,
O'er Hills, and sinking Bogs, and pathless Downs.
Of Stars he told that shoot with shining Trail,
And of the Glow-worms Light that gilds his Tail.
He sung where Wood-cocks in the Summer feed,
And in what Climates they renew their Breed;

Line
47. *Nec tantum Phœbo gaudet Parnasia rupes*
Nec tantum Rhodope mirantur & Ismarus Orphea.   Virg.
51. *Our Swain had probably read* Tusser *from whence he might have collected these Philosophical Observations.*
Namque canebat uti magnum per inane coacta, &c.   Virg.
                                              Some

Some think to Northern Coasts their Flight they tend,
Or to the Moon in Midnight Hours ascend.
Where Swallows in the Winter's Season keep, 65
And how the drowsie Bat and Dormouse sleep.
How Nature does the Puppy's Eyelid close,
'Till the bright Sun has nine times set and rose.
For Huntsmen by their long Experience find,
That Puppys still nine rolling Suns are blind. 70

Now he goes on, and sings of Fairs and Shows,
For still new Fairs before his Eyes arose.
How Pedlars Stalls with glitt'ring Toys are laid,
The various Fairings of the Country Maid.
Long silken Laces hang upon the Twine, 75
And Rows of Pins and amber Bracelets shine;
How the tight Lass, Knives, Combs and Scissars spys,
And looks on Thimbles with desiring Eyes.
Of Lott'ries next with tuneful Note he told,
Where silver Spoons are won and Rings of Gold.
The Lads and Lasses trudge the Street along, 81
And all the Fair is crouded in his Song.

The

The Mountebank now treads the Stage, and sells

His Pills, his Balsoms, and his Ague spells;

Now o'er and o'er the nimble Tumbler springs, 85

And on the Rope the vent'rous Maiden swings;

Jack-pudding in his parti-coloured Jacket

Tosses the Glove and jokes at ev'ry Packet.

Of *Raree-Shows* he sung, and *Punch's* Feats,

Of Pockets pick'd in Crowds, and various Cheats.

Then sad he sung *the Children in the Wood.*   91

Ah barb'rous Uncle, stain'd with Infant Blood!

How Blackberrys they pluck'd in Desarts wild,

And fearless at the glittering Fauchion smil'd;

Their little Corps the Robin-red-breasts found, 95

And strow'd with pious Bill the Leaves around.

Ah gentle Birds! if this Verse lasts so long,

Your Names shall live for ever in my Song.

For Buxom *Joan* he sung the doubtful Strife,

How the sly Sailor made the Maid a Wife.   100

Line

97. *Fortunati ambo, si quid mea Carmina possunt,*
Nulla Dies unquam memori vos eximet ævo.   Virg.

99. *A Song in the Comedy of* Love for Love, *beginning* A Soldier and a
Sailor, *&c.*

To louder Strains he rais'd his Voice, to tell
What woeful Wars in *Chevy-Chace* befell,
When *Piercy drove the Deer with Hound and Horn,*
Wars to be wept by Children yet unborn!   104
Ah *With'rington*, more Years thy Life had crown'd,
If thou had'ſt never heard the Horn or Hound!
Yet ſhall the Squire, who fought on bloody Stumps,
By future Bards be wail'd in doleful Dumps.

All in the Land of Eſſex next he chaunts,   109
How to ſleek Mares ſtarch Quakers turn Gallants;
How the grave Brother ſtood on Bank ſo green.
Happy for him if Mares had never been!

Then he was ſeiz'd with a religious Qualm,
And on a ſudden, ſung the hundredth Pſalm.

He ſung of *Taffey-Welch,* and *Sawney Scot,*
Lilly-bullero and the *Iriſh Trot.*

Line
109. *A Song of Sir* J. Denham's. *See his Poems.*
112. *Et fortunatam ſi nunquam Armenta fuiſſent*
     Paſiphaen.   Virg.

Why fhould I tell of *Bateman* or of *Shore*,
Or *Wantley*'s *Dragon* flain by valiant *Moore*,
The Bow'r of Rofamond, or *Robin Hood*,   119
And how the *Grafs now grows where* Troy Town *ſtood?*

    His Carrols ceas'd : The liſt'ning Maids and Swains
Seem ſtill to hear ſome ſoft imperfect Strains.
Sudden he roſe; and as he reels along
Swears Kiſſes ſweet ſhould well reward his Song.
The Damſels laughing fly : the giddy Clown   125
Again upon a Wheat-Sheaf drops adown;
The Pow'r that Guards the Drunk, his Sleep attends,
'Till, ruddy, like his Face, the Sun deſcends.

Line
117. *Quid loquar aut Scyllam Niſi*, &c. Virg.
117. *Old Engliſh Ballads.*

An

An Alphabetical Catalogue of *Names*, Plants, Flowers, Fruits, Birds, Beasts, Insects and other material Things mentioned by this Author.

INDEX.

INDEX.

INDEX.

FINIS.